MANAGEMENT

An
Experiential
Approach

MANAGEMENT

An
Experiential
Approach

LAWRENCE R. JAUCH
Northeast Louisiana University

SALLY A. COLTRIN
University of North Florida

THE DRYDEN PRESS
Harcourt Brace College Publishers
Chicago   New York San Francisco Philadelphia
Montreal Toronto London Sydney Tokyo

Address for Editorial Correspondence
The Dryden Press, 301 Commerce Street, Suite 3700, Fort Worth, TX 76102

Address for Orders
The Dryden Press, 6277 Sea Harbor Drive, Orlando, FL 32887
1-800-782-4479, or 1-800-433-0001 (in Florida)

ISBN: 0-03-097520-4

Printed in the United States of America

3 4 5 6 7 8 9 0 1 2 085 9 8 7 6 5 4 3 2 1

The Dryden Press
Harcourt Brace College Publishers

PREFACE

Welcome to a set of exercises that provide a new managerial experience. The following pages present a variety of exercises that we hope you will find interesting and valuable. These materials are designed as an aid to supplement your basic knowledge of the management field.

Our two major objectives in the preparation of this supplement were to promote skill development in the areas of leadership, communication, decision making, planning, and organizational design; and to increase your understanding of the manager's job and environment, individual and group behavior, and staffing, conflict, control, and change processes. This understanding will help you effectively apply the managerial skills you will learn.

You will be asked to think about managerial problems, make decisions, interview managers, and discuss various issues with your peers. Your understanding of management will be enhanced by active participation in the process you are about to undertake.

This supplement contains three kinds of exercises: field, individual, and small group. The field exercises ask you to interview a manager or visit an organization to gain insight into how managers function and how the organization operates. Individual exercises are those you can complete on your own but that may be discussed in class. Some of the exercises will be valuable to your own career and personal development in addition to helping you develop an understanding of basic managerial concepts. The group exercises (some of which relate to the individual exercises) are designed to give you experience in working with others toward a common goal and an understanding of how others' perceptions and approaches to problems may differ from yours.

Although you may not be assigned all the exercises included in the book, we hope you will be stimulated to complete some of them on your own. Your interest in management and your ability to comprehend the world of the manager will be increased to the extent that you are involved with these situations. We trust that you will have a rewarding managerial experience.

We sincerely appreciate the cooperation of the authors and publishers who granted us permission to incorporate their material into this volume. Of course, we are responsible for any omissions or errors in content. We hope the material included will help you develop your skills and understanding of the managerial job and stimulate your interest in a career in management.

Lawrence R. Jauch
Monroe, Louisiana

Sally A. Coltrin
Jacksonville, Florida

Arthur G. Bedeian
Baton Rouge, Louisiana

April, 1993

CONTENTS

REDUCING FUD: THE PICTURE PROJECT

In the world of work, managers get the job done through people. These people often work together in groups. Humans have found through the ages that organizations are a superior way to accomplish goals. Historians think that one of Egypt's pharaohs assembled over 20,000 workers to build his pyramid. Native Americans formed tribes for protection and improved hunting techniques.

Cooperative endeavors involving work teams often improve the performance of individuals. Have you ever tried making a king-sized bed by yourself? You have to keep walking from side to side to smooth out the bedsheets, tuck in the blankets, straighten the pillows, and put on the bedcover. When two people cooperate in such a task, the job is easier and quicker than it would be if each were to do it independently.

When you enter a new workplace, you will find yourself working with others. As a manager you will have to acquaint yourself with strangers before you can become a part of an efficient and effective work group. Anyone entering a new job will experience FUD—fear, uncertainty and doubt. Can I do the work? How will coworkers react to me? What will they be like?

This exercise is designed to help you acquaint yourself with other members of a group who are also experiencing FUD. You may be asked to work together in a variety of other tasks and exercises you will be doing as you learn about the jobs of managers. Your instructor will guide you as you enter into this first managerial experience—reducing FUD as you enter into a new group.

To do this exercise, show up in class with a small (2" x 3") recent photograph of yourself—your instructor will give you other directions.

Exercise 1 UNDERSTANDING MANAGERIAL JOBS

The ten managerial roles described by Henry Mintzberg are the basis of this exercise. You should have a good understanding of Mintzberg's ten roles for this exercise. Your assignment is to interview a manager and compare your findings with others in the class.

Find a plant manager, foreman, hospital administrator, store owner, or the like, whose job primarily involves supervising the work of other people or running an enterprise. (Your subject may be chosen from business, public or private agencies, schools, and so forth.) Your goal is to obtain the following information:

a. Which of the ten roles are most important? Which contribute to effective performance by this manager?

b. Which of the ten roles are most time-consuming?

c. Which examples of the roles can be provided by this manager?

In conducting your interview, you may find the following questions helpful (but you may add your own):

1. What is your official title?

2. What do you do in a normal work day? For example, describe what you did yesterday.

3. What off-the-job duties are involved in your work?

4. Are you active in community or social clubs? Do they help you with your job?

5. What kinds of problems do you have to solve on the job? How do you handle the problems that arise?

6. With whom do you eat lunch? Do you entertain work associates?

7. How do you get subordinates to produce?

The ten roles are listed on the following pages. Based on the information from your interview, complete the Manager's Role Profile. Enter the appropriate numbers for each role based on the following scales:

Column A:

(1) role not important

(2) of minimal importance

(3) of some importance

(4) of considerable importance

(5) of very high importance (that is, important for effective job performance)

Column B:

(1) no time consumed

(2) minimal time consumed

(3) some time consumed

(4) considerable time consumed

(5) very high amount of time consumed (that is, time consumed in performing the job)

Example: Provide an example of this role from the work of the manager.

Fill in Columns A and B for every job role, even if you have difficulty identifying an example. Arrange your interview so that you gather information on which to base the numerical answers for each role.

You might then examine your data to see if interpersonal roles, informational roles, or decisional roles are more important to effectiveness, and which of these consumes the most time.

You may be asked to report your findings for class discussion and comparison with others' findings about differences along such dimensions as job level in the hierarchy, type of firm, and so forth.

A MANAGER'S ROLE PROFILE

(to be completed after the interview)

Position _____Industry _____

Level in hierarchy _____   Size of enterprise _____
(Top, middle, low)   (Number of employees)

Roles the manager performs:

Column A. How important is this to effective job performance? (1–5)
Column B. How time consuming is this role? (1–5)

                                                                   A   B

A.   Interpersonal roles

    1. Figurehead: duties of a ceremonial nature; somewhat routine; little serious communication (dinners, dances, civic meetings, etc.)

       Example: _____   _____

    2. Leader: direct leadership; motivation and employee supervision; staffing and training (develops people, selects personnel, influences employees)

       Example: _____   _____

    3. Liaison: makes contacts outside the vertical chain of command (staff meetings; luncheons with peers, clients, suppliers, government, etc.)

       Example: _____   _____

B.   Information roles

    4. Monitor: scanning the environment for information; nerve center for the organization (interrogates liaison contacts and subordinates, reviews reports)

       Example: _____   _____

	A	B

5 Disseminator: passes along privileged information to subordinates (meetings, memos, letters, and briefings with subordinates)

Example:

6. Spokesperson: passes along information to people outside the organization (uses liaison contacts,speaks to groups, talks to suppliers and salespeople, communicates to stockholders and directors)

Example:

C.   Decisional Roles

7. Entrepreneur: adapts and changes organization to fit the environment; initiates project development (cost reduction programs, departmental reorganization, public relations campaign, development of forecasting system)

Example:

8. Disturbance handler: involuntary response to pressure; takes corrective action on problems (reacts to strikes or grievance policy on bankrupt customer, responds to supplier who reneges on contract)

Example:

9. Resource allocator: deciding which organizational units receive which resources; authorizes budgets and major decisions (assigns personnel, sets objectives, makes capital expenditure decisions, schedules work)

Example:

10. Negotiator: represents organization in negotiating with employees, suppliers, customers; negotiates with other departments (resolves jurisdictional disputes, hires key personnel, negotiates sale or union contracts)

Example:

DEVELOPING QUALITY CONTROL PROCEDURES IN A PARTICIPATIVE MANNER

You are a member of Darton, Denton, and Ferbes, Consultants, a new organization in the areas of managerial and marketing consulting, with no control procedures to evaluate the quality of services it offers its clients. Its clients consist primarily of large- and middle-sized organizations—mainly banks and export marketers—in a large eastern port city.

Darton, Denton, and Ferbes has a staff of five consultants, including Messrs. Darton and Denton and Mrs. Ferbes. Messrs. Darton and Denton, both in their fifties, are MBAs who retired early and sought new careers. Mr. Darton, a retired colonel, was an operations research consultant in the Army, responsible for equipment supply operations in Europe. Mr. Denton, retired from International Foods, was vice-president and director of marketing. Mrs. Ferbes, aged forty-seven, operated her own bank consulting business in Chicago for twenty years. Her husband was transferred, and Mrs. Ferbes looked for a new position in consulting. Darton, Denton, and Ferbes hired two additional employees—Jack Fraiser and Timothy O'Dell. Jack holds a bachelor's degree in finance and would like to get an MBA, but he is only twenty-one and would like to get some experience before going back to school. Tim, aged twenty-nine, went on to get his MBA after undergraduate school and a stint in the Air Force. He has a bachelor's degree in management and an MBA in accounting and worked for two years as an accountant.

Darton, Denton, and Ferbes has been consulting for two years and has managed to obtain eight major accounts on a continuing basis and approximately thirty accounts on a noncontinuous basis. Annual gross billings for last year were $755,000, with an approximate return on investment of 9 percent. Gross billings for the first quarter of this year were $207,625.

DDF limits its accounts to specific areas of managerial and marketing consulting. For example, the consultants work closely with bank and export company personnel departments to study hiring and training procedures. It also studies employee movement patterns within a bank or company and the reasons why employees resign. From its analyses, DDF makes suggestions for personnel policies. Additionally, it studies the size of the organization in relation to its product or service and environment and makes recommendations for changes in the organizational structure. It will advise on one-time, noncontinuous problems of the type discussed above.

DDF's marketing consulting consists mainly of helping export companies with their foreign distribution problems. For example, moving products to coastal areas in the Middle East is easy; however, distributing these products to the interior is hindered by lack of transportation facilities, perishability of products, and inability of U.S. exporters to communicate with members of Middle Eastern cultures. DDF also assists banks' newly formed marketing departments in advertising. Banks, in a highly competitive industry, have found the need for more and continued advertising research but do not feel qualified to handle the function themselves. DDF has contracted with one bank group and several savings and loan institutions to carry out advertising research on a continuing basis. It also has several one-time commitments to evaluate the effectiveness of advertising programs in smaller cities near its home office.

6

Mr. Darton, the company's president, plans to call a meeting of all his consultants to address the issue of quality controls for the consulting being done by Darton, Denton, and Ferbes. Although he has some ideas of his own, he does not plan to set forth controls at this time. Instead, he will request that each of you come to the meeting prepared to discuss quality controls that can be implemented.

Your instructor will divide the class into groups of five. Each person will be assigned to play the role of one of the consultants described in the exercise. Before this exercise is discussed in class, think from the perspective of the role you are playing about what quality control processes could and should be implemented in the organization. During the first part of the class period your group will discuss ideas and develop a quality control plan. Each group will then present its plan to the class for further discussion.

Your instructor may give you additional guidelines.

Exercise 3

A UNIVERSITY'S ENVIRONMENT

Almost every organization, regardless of its type or nature, must be concerned with the external environmental influences that impinge upon it. This exercise is designed to provide you with an opportunity to evaluate the external environmental elements that influence an organization with which you are presently associated—your university.

Either individuals or small groups, as designated by your instructor, will be assigned the responsibility of interviewing one of the following persons in the university community to discuss the effects of the environment on university operations:

1. Vice-president for Academic Affairs
2. Vice-president for Business Affairs (or a high-ranking financial officer)
3. Vice-president (or Dean) of Students or Student Affairs
4. Vice-president or Director of University Relations (such as the Public Relations Officer)
5. Purchasing Agent
6. Director of Admissions
7. Director of Alumni Association

Your instructor may suggest additional or substitute persons to be interviewed. Questions you should focus on are:

1. What groups comprise a university's environment?
2. In what ways does each element of the environment affect the organization?
3. How does the environmental composition vary, based upon whether the school is public or private?
4. How do the internal variables of volatility, size, complexity, and objectives influence how critical external factors are to the school? Cite examples to substantiate your response to this question.
5. Based upon your research in this exercise, do university administrators act primarily as spokespersons or negotiators in their relationships with the environment?

Each person or group will be responsible for making a brief report to the class outlining its findings. The collective results should provide the basis for a complete evaluation of the environmental influences. Your instructor will give you additional specific instructions.

WOULD YOU DO THAT?

Below is a list of behaviors that you or your peers might engage in when working for a company. Go through each item and circle the number that best indicates the frequency with which you personally would (or do, if you work now) engage in this behavior.

1. Do your colleagues do these things more often than you do?
2. Which behaviors are more prone to be done more often?
3. How are these different from the behaviors done less frequently

Bring your results to class for discussion.

Behavior	At Every Opportunity	Often	About Half the Time	Seldom	Never
1. Passing blame for errors to an innocent co-worker	5	4	3	2	1
2. Divulging confidential information	5	4	3	2	1
3. Falsifying time/quality/quantity reports	5	4	3	2	1
4. Claiming credit for someone else's work	5	4	3	2	1
5. Padding an expense account over 10 percent	5	4	3	2	1
6. Pilfering company materials and supplies	5	4	3	2	1
7. Accepting gifts/favors in exchange for preferential treatment	5	4	3	2	1
8. Giving gifts/favors in exchange for preferential treatment	5	4	3	2	1
9. Padding an expense account up to 10 percent	5	4	3	2	1
10. Authorizing a subordinate to violate company rules	5	4	3	2	1
11. Calling in sick to take a day off	5	4	3	2	1
12. Concealing one's errors	5	4	3	2	1
13. Taking longer than necessary to do a job	5	4	3	2	1
14. Using company services for personal use	5	4	3	2	1
15. Doing personal business on company time	5	4	3	2	1
16. Taking extra personal time (lunch hour, breaks, early departure, and so forth)	5	4	3	2	1
17. Not reporting others' violations of company policies and rules	5	4	3	2	1
18. Overlooking a superior's violation of policy to prove loyalty to the boss	5	4	3	2	1

Source: Adapted by Lawrence R. Jauch from John W. Newstrom and William A. Ruch, "The Ethics of Management and the Management of Ethics," p. 35, *MSU Business Topics,* Winter 1975. Reprinted by permission of the publisher, Division of Research, Graduate School of Business Administration, Michigan State University.

Exercise 5 | PLANNING FOR THE FUTURE

The makeup of the population of a given society, changes taking place in the size and shape of that population, and the effects those changes are likely to have is the subject of demography. Managers and planners need to pay attention to these changes and forecast their potential implications because they are likely to have a significant impact on their business and careers.

This exercise provides you with an opportunity to gather some data, assess the impact it may have on your future, and plan for it.

First, read the background information. Then gather the data suggested and answer the questions at the end of the exercise. Bring your findings to class for discussion.

BACKGROUND INFORMATION

What happened to Gerber Products? Why did it add new products beyond its baby food line? American Hospital Supply Company has grown at a phenomenal rate lately. Why? Part of the answer to these questions is: The baby boom has become a baby bust. After a steady decline in the U.S. birthrate from the 1800s to 1940, a twenty-year period of increased birthrate occurred, going from about two to four children per woman. This was followed by a decline in the 1960s and 1970s. The birthrate (among other variables) has an impact on total population size and affects age range proportions; these in turn affect basic patterns for certain goods and services.

Another significant feature of birthrate data is the number of families without children. A two-paycheck family with no children results in different housing patterns, disposable income, and consumption patterns to life-style differences. A nation where the average family has two children will have a higher per capita income than one where the average family has three. Disposable income would increase and be used for travel, entertainment, or a vacation home. People won't eat more, but they might eat more convenience and gourmet foods, or dine out more often.

The work force, meanwhile, also begins to take on a different composition. The post–World War II baby boom meant more people competing for middle management positions in the 1980s and 1990s. With fewer in schools, thousands of teachers were competing for jobs also. A smaller group of young people growing up after the baby boom generation may see a perpetual barrier for success and prosperity. However, scarcity of young people may also mean they are in demand for jobs requiring youthful energy and fresh training. Demand for specialists may also change. For example, while there may be an oversupply of physicians, there may be less need for obstetricians and more need for specialists in geriatric care.

What some have come to call the "graying of America" could have significant impact on demand patterns for products and services, and threats and opportunities for various segments of the economy in the future. Birthrate data and age composition of the population can give significant clues to the patterns which could emerge in the future, affecting businesses and their managers in predictable ways. This exercise seeks to stimulate your thinking about these patterns and their implications for you and your future planning.

YOUR ASSIGNMENT

1. Gather basic data on the population. Your library should have census data collected by the government. The Statistical Abstract of the United States provides convenient reference data.

2. Draw a series of bar charts with respect to trends for each decade from 1900 through 1990 (every ten years) for the following:

   a. Total population

   b. Number of men and women

   c. Children born per woman (births, rates, fertility)

   d. Percent of population by age category:

      (1) 1–13 (2) 14–21 (3) 22–34 (4) 35–65 (5) over 65

3. For each of the following categories of economic activity, indicate what your data suggests. (Check whether the segment will be hurt or helped, and provide a brief explanation indicating which of your charts leads you to conclude that the segment will be hurt or helped.)

Economic Segment	Helped	Hurt	Why? What chart supports it?
Advertising			
Autos			
Broadcasting			
Clothing			
Health Care			
Housing			
Jewelry, watches			
Life insurance			
Liquor			
Movie theatres			
Restaurants			
Tobacco			
Travel			

4. Comment on how these data are likely to affect you as a manager, or how planners should respond in each segment.

5. Bring your findings to class to discuss and compare.

| |

Exercise 6 | **STRATEGIC DECISIONS FOR THE TUCKER COMPANY**

This exercise is designed to help you learn how individuals and groups might choose among alternative strategies for their organization.

First, read the background information of the Tucker Company on your own. Then, individually, complete Table 6–1, Individual Resource Distribution. Next, read the section on strategic alternatives, and complete Table 6–2, Individual Strategic Resource Distribution. Finally, meet with your team to make decisions about Table 6–3, Group Strategic Resource Distribution. After you have completed the three tables, work on the Analysis Section.

TUCKER COMPANY BACKGROUND INFORMATION

The Tucker Company is a well-regarded medium-sized food processing company located in central Ohio. Its major orientation is the production and marketing of jams, jellies, and ice cream toppings in the United States and Canada. Tucker is fairly well established in about two-thirds of the major markets, and sells through food and discount wholesalers and retailers. Tucker maintains one plant in Ohio and has contracts for fruit and other raw materials (e.g., sugar, syrup, glass containers, etc.) with a variety of suppliers.

The company has justifiably earned a reputation for producing high-quality food products. Over the past few years, Tucker has enjoyed a 10 percent annual gain in sales and earnings in the products and markets they now serve. This has been accomplished without significant investments in research and development, new products, or production improvements for the past ten years.

The Tucker family, owners of the company, have indicated a willingness to explore a number of alternative growth possibilities for the future. They have hired you as a consultant to assist them in making strategic decisions with regard to how they should invest in the future. The feeling is that to sustain growth, the company is at the point where some investment needs to be made.

Capital is not a constraint. Through retained earnings and a good line of credit, Tucker Company is capable of investing in several projects. The owners, however, do wish to use their capital wisely to produce a greater return than that which is being achieved now.

As a consultant, you have been asked to plan the priority of the investments you think the company should pursue. The owners suggest that you consider allocating funds to the following five strategic alternatives:

1. Increase penetration of existing markets.
2. Increase number of markets served.
3. Extend vertically forward (closer to the final consumer).
4. Extend vertically backward (basic raw materials).
5. Expand production capacity.

Given these five strategic alternatives, you should indicate in Table 6–1 how you would prefer to allocate the resources available to the Tucker Company. Assuming that total resources equal 100 percent, distribute your allocation to each of the five alternatives in any manner you prefer such that they add up to 100 percent. You must allocate something to each alternative. Your distribution should reflect the importance you feel each should have in terms of its contribution to overall development and goals of the company.

14

TABLE 6–1

INDIVIDUAL RESOURCE DISTRIBUTION

Strategic Alternative	Resource Allocation
1. Increase penetration of existing markets	_____ %
2. Increase number of markets served	_____ %
3. Extend vertically forward	_____ %
4. Extend vertically backward	_____ %
5. Expand production capacity	_____ %
Total	100 %

Your consulting firm has explored the five strategic alternatives in greater detail with company executives and industry experts. Two options (I and II) have been identified as potential ways to implement each of the five strategic alternatives. After reading each option for each alternative, indicate how you would allocate resources among each option on Table 6–2. You may allot 100 percent to I and 0 percent to II, or vice versa; or you may use any combination of resources (e.g., 50–50, 70–30, 15–85, etc.), as long as the resources allocated to the two options equal 100 percent for each alternative.

If you allocate less than 100 percent to either option, it may result in less than optimum returns for that particular option. The returns are assumed to be relatively proportional to the amount invested. However, 100 percent allocation to either option does not necessarily automatically assure full accomplishment of that option.

Option I   **Option II**

1. Increase penetration of existing markets

Add sales personnel and promotional efforts in existing markets.Focus on those products(jams and jellies) that contribute greatest profit margin. There is a high probability that this effort can increase demand for currently profitable products.

Introduce new lines of products (honey, peanut butter, jelly combination) into existing markets. The company image may lead to consumer acceptance and, if successful, high profitability. Consumer acceptance of these higher-priced convenience products is subject to uncertain economic conditions.

2. Increase number of markets served

Using existing product lines, invest in promotion in major domestic markets not now served. Market research suggests demand in some major markets may justify this activity and would help growth in sales. Return on investment will be roughly the same as in current markets, but volume will be higher.

Using existing product lines and possibly one new line, begin processing and promotion in selected foreign markets. The returns of this strategy are likely to be high with relatively low volume. However, the instability in the countries involved may result in takeover or control of processing plants.

3. Extend vertically forward (closer to the final consumer)

Invest in small retail outlets (24-hour convenience stores) which handle limited product lines including Tucker products. This could result in increased sales, but future growth potential of these outlets is limited.

Buy out or merge with some of the wholesalers who deal in Tucker products as well as products of other food processors. Expertise in wholesaling is not currently one of Tucker's strengths, but control over these distributors could result in a considerably higher rate of return.

4. Extend vertically backward (closer to basic raw materials)

There is an opportunity to invest in the development of three or four of the orchards owned by major fruit suppliers used in toppings, jellies, and jams. Tucker currently employs inspectors who have technical competence in cultivating and harvesting these fruits. Control of these raw materials would help smooth fluctuations in product availability and cost.

Acquire or merge with the major glass works that provides jars and bottles for packaging jams and jellies. Very significant cost savings could be achieved in total product cost with control over this resource. Technology and management know-how in this field are not possessed by Tucker, and the glass company has been owned by the same family firm for eighty years.

5. Expand production capacity

Some processing efficiencies could result from investment in more modern processing equipment and procedures in the production of jams and jellies. A reduction in amount of product inspection would also result in increased plant output without significant losses in product quality (although the "Grade A Fancy" rating from USDA may become only "Grade A").

Invest in new plants located closer to sources of raw materials (orchards). There is some concern that if an orchard fails due to unfavorable climatic conditions, severe inefficiencies and plant closings could result. (Crop failure occurs every four or five years.) At the same time, transportation costs can be significantly reduced, yielding much higher profitability.

At this point, you should meet with a study group and make group decisions about how you would allocate resources among the strategic alternatives. And, within each alternative, decide how your group wants to allocate resources between the two options. Discuss each alternative and option completely before deciding on your allocation. Follow the procedures you used individually, and place your decisions in Table 6–3.

TABLE 6–2
INDIVIDUAL STRATEGIC RESOURCE DISTRIBUTION

Strategic Alternative	Option I	Option II	Total
1. Increase penetration of existing markets	_____ %	_____ %	100%
2. Increase number of markets served	_____ %	_____ %	100%
3. Extend vertically forward	_____ %	_____ %	100%
4. Extend vertically backward	_____ %	_____ %	100%
5. Expand production capacity	_____ %	_____ %	100%

16

TABLE 6–3
GROUP STRATEGIC DISTRIBUTION

Strategic Alternative	Resource Allocation among Alternatives	Opt. I	Opt. II	Total
1. Increase penetration of existing markets	_____ %	_____ %	_____ %	100%
2. Increase number of markets served	_____ %	_____ %	_____ %	100%
3. Extend vertically forward	_____ %	_____ %	_____ %	100%
4. Extend vertically backward	_____ %	_____ %	_____ %	100%
5. Expand production capacity	100%	_____ %	_____ %	100%

ANALYSIS

Do a little introspection. When confronted with decision situations, are you a risk seeker or risk averter? Do you seek out and make decisions which expose you to a high degree of risk in situations which you are uncertain about? In these instances, there might be a high payoff or high loss. Are you willing to take such a chance? Or do you seek to minimize loss and play it "close to the vest"? For example, if you play poker, are you often willing to gamble on a bluff or draw to a hand that has a low probability of success but possibly high payoff (risk seeker); or would you fold a hand and not risk further losses (risk averter)?

In the space below, indicate whether you are a risk seeker or a risk averter. If you avoid risk in most or all situations, pick a number closer to 0. If you are a high risk taker, choose a number closer to 100. Cross out the box which best describes your approach to risky situations.

Risk Averter | 0 | 10 | 20 | 30 | 40 | 50 | 60 | 70 | 80 | 90 | 100 | **Risk Seeker**

This is your "individual risk estimate."

To help you analyze your actual attitudes toward risk taking, complete Tables 6–4 and 6–5.

In Table 6–4, enter in Column 1 the values you individually decided upon for each strategic alternative in Table 6–1. In Column 2, enter the values you decided upon for Option II in Table 6–2. Multiply Columns 1 and 2 and enter the product in Column 3. At the bottom of that column, add the column total, then divide by 100 for your "individual risk attitude." In Column 4, enter the values your group decided upon (from Table 6–3) for allocation among the strategic alternatives. In Column 5, enter the values your group chose for Option II in Table 6–3. Column 6 is the product of Columns 4 and 5. At the bottom of Column 6 total the values, then divide by 100 for your "group risk attitude." You may have noted that Option II for each strategic alternative was more risky than Option I.

In Table 6–5, for each member of your group, enter the "individual risk estimates" in Column 1 and enter the "individual risk attitude" (from Table 6–4, Column 3) in Column 2. Find the average of these two columns. At the bottom of Column 2 enter the "group risk attitude" (From Table 6–4, Column 6).

You may wish to explore what differences exist within your group, and why these occur.

TABLE 6–4
ATTITUDES TOWARD RISK

	INDIVIDUAL		
	Col. 1 % Alloc. to Alternative	Col. 2 Option II Alloc.	Col. 3 (1) x (2)
1. Penetrate existing markets	_____	_____	_____
2. Increase number of markets	_____	_____	_____
3. Extend vertically forward	_____	_____	_____
4. Extend vertically backward	_____	_____	_____
5. Expand production capacity	_____	_____	_____
		Sum =	_____
		Individual risk attitude	
		Sum/100 =	_____

	GROUP		
	Col. 4 % Alloc. to Alternative	Col. 5 Option II Alloc.	Col. 6 (4) x (5)
1. Penetrate existing markets	_____	_____	_____
2. Increase number of markets	_____	_____	_____
3. Extend vertically forward	_____	_____	_____
4. Extend vertically backward	_____	_____	_____
5. Expand production capacity	_____	_____	_____
		Sum =	_____
		Group risk attitude	
		Sum/100 =	_____

TABLE 6–5
RISK ESTIMATES AND ATTITUDE COMPARISONS

Group Member	Col. 1 Individual Risk Estimate	Col. 2 Individual Risk Attitude
_____	_____	_____
_____	_____	_____
_____	_____	_____
_____	_____	_____
_____	_____	_____
_____	_____	_____
_____	_____	_____
_____	_____	_____
Average	_____	_____ (A)
Group risk attitude	_____	_____ (B)

Exercise 7 — PRESTIGIOUS OCCUPATIONS

Below is a list of fifteen occupations of possibly varying prestige. We want your personal opinion on the general standing of each job. Your individual results will be compared with those of others in class and with a national sample of the American adult population. First, read the directions below and complete the form independently. Your task is to rank these fifteen occupations in the same order of prestige as the sample of the American public did. Place the number 1 by the occupation that you think was ranked as the most prestigious by the national sample; place the number 2 by the second most prestigious occupation, and so on through number 15, which would be your estimate of the least prestigious of the fifteen occupations.

Occupation	
Priest	_____
Nuclear physicist	_____
Author of novels	_____
Banker	_____
Member of a board of directors of a large corporation	_____
Carpenter	_____
Owner of a factory that employs about 100 people	_____
Physician	_____
Electrician	_____
Lawyer	_____
Architect	_____
College professor	_____
Official of an international labor union	_____
State governor	_____
Undertaker	_____

Your instructor will ask you to form small groups and give you directions to complete this exercise. Leave this page blank until you receive instructions on its completion. It is to be used for a group decision.

Carpenter	_____
Owner of a factory that employs about 100 people	_____
Physician	_____
Electrician	_____
Lawyer	_____
Architect	_____
College professor	_____
Official of an international labor union	_____
State governor	_____
Undertaker	_____
Priest	_____
Nuclear physicist	_____
Author of novels	_____
Banker	_____
Member of a board of directors of a large corporation	_____

Exercise 8 | RESTRUCTURING THE UNIVERSITY

Midwestern State University is faced with the need to reduce its budget. All of the "easy" actions such as eliminating travel budgets, leaving open positions unfilled, and trimming operating expenses have been implemented. The university has a student population of 14,500, plus 1,500 graduate students, mostly in education. The undergraduate distribution is as follows:

Business	4,500
Natural Sciences	1,500
Humanities	1,750
Law Enforcement	2,000
Allied Health	750
Other	4,000
Graduate (all)	1,500

The administration is looking at reorganization possibilities as a means of achieving the revised budget goals. However, the Board of Regents (the school's governing body) has made the following stipulations:

1. The numbers of currently employed teaching faculty must not be reduced.
2. No increase in the numbers of administrative personnel or staff may be made.
3. No one can become unemployed, however their positions and responsibilities may be changed.
4. No existing program may be put in a position of losing its accreditation.

The academic vice-president is charged with determining and implementing the necessary changes to reduce the academic budget by the maximum amount possible. The current structure of the university is shown in Figure 8–1. A more detailed presentation of the College of Business (Figure 8–2), College of Allied Health (Figure 8–3) and College of Natural Sciences (Figure 8–4) are also given. Additional information about the current university structure and detailed discussions of the program offerings are presented below. In addition to the three schools listed above, the university also has a College of Humanities and Social Sciences, a College of Education, a College of Health and Recreation, a College of Law Enforcement which also offers first-aid courses, and a Graduate School. The normal teaching load is four sections and, depending on the size of class sections, anywhere from two to four preparations. Administrators at the department chair level receive an additional $1,500 in salary and a reduction in course load to two sections, plus the additional summer salary they would normally be paid for teaching two courses during the summer, but without responsibility for teaching those courses. Deans are on twelve-month appointments and receive $50,000 per year. They are required to teach one course each year. Summer salaries are set as follows:

Instructor	$1,700
Assistant Professor	$2,100
Associate Professor	$2,400
Full Professor	$2,700

Source: Adapted from "Restructuring the University," ABSEL Proceedings, 1990, by permission of Eric Panitz.

EXHIBIT 8–1

STRUCTURE OF THE UNIVERSITY

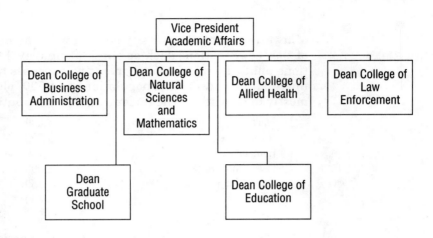

EXHIBIT 8–2

STRUCTURE OF THE COLLEGE OF BUSINESS

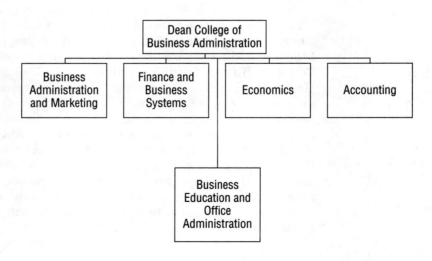

EXHIBIT 8–3
STRUCTURE OF THE COLLEGE OF ALLIED HEALTH

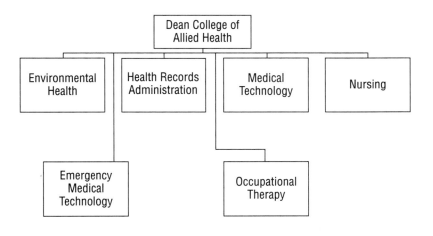

EXHIBIT 8–4
STRUCTURE OF THE COLLEGE OF NATURAL SCIENCES

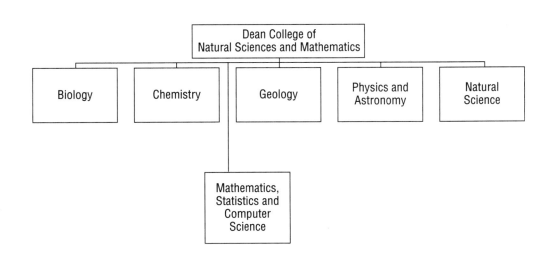

THE COLLEGE OF BUSINESS ADMINISTRATION

This school consists of five departments and thirteen programs. Several programs have specified options which enable a student to concentrate in a specific area such as computer programming as opposed to management information systems. The programs offered are summarized below. Many students in the Allied Health and Natural Sciences are required to take some of the business core courses as part of their major or minor programs. A specific example of this is the Principles of Management course required of Health Records Administration majors.

Department of Business Administration and Marketing

This department houses the management, marketing, general business, and coal mining administration programs. The faculty totals 17: four are in the management area, four are in marketing, three teach in the coal mining administration program, and six teach in general business.

Management offers three options:

Business Administration—designed to train students to become mid-level managers and occupy staff supervisory positions.

Industrial Relations—designed to develop skills in personnel administration, organization development, and human resource management.

Operations Management—designed to develop skills in production management, quality control, inventory, and operations research.

Marketing offers two options:

Marketing—qualifies students for positions in sales and sales management, retailing, marketing research, promotion, and advertising.

Transportation—develops students to enter the field of transportation and physical distribution management.

Coal Mining Administration qualifies students to enter managerial positions in the coal industry such as mine administrative positions, reclamation work, and occupational safety as related to the mining industry.

General Business offers courses in law, the capstone policy course, and courses in small business administration. There is also a major in general business designed for students planning to attend professional or graduate schools.

Department of Finance and Business Information Systems

This department houses 16 faculty members, four in each of the following areas: management information systems and programming, finance, insurance, and real estate.

MIS/EDP—trains students in business and applications of programming, and management information systems development and management.

Finance—provides students with tools of effective decision making for careers in corporate finance, banking, and investment firms and agencies.

Insurance—provides students with background for entering careers in the insurance industry and for attaining CLU and CPCU certifications.

Real Estate—develops students' capabilities in real estate management, marketing, appraisal, finance, and property management and development.

Department of Economics

This department has eleven faculty members who teach largely introductory economics and business statistics courses. Advanced courses are offered to all majors in the School of Business. Economics majors are offered both through the School of Business and the College of Humanities.

Department of Accounting

This department contains eleven faculty members who teach the introductory accounting courses to all majors and business minors. There are two majors offered through the department:

Accounting—a major in accounting is prepared to seek the CPA certification and for accounting positions in government or industry.

Health Care Administration—specific training for positions in hospital administration is offered in a cooperative program with the College of Allied Health.

Department of Business Education and Office Administration

This department has eight faculty who teach business communications courses for all majors, and office management, secretarial, and business education courses to their respective majors.

Office Administration—provides office personnel to fill responsible positions in business and industry as executive secretaries, administrative assistants, and other similar positions.

Secretarial Program—a two-year degree program designed to train legal, medical, and executive secretaries in office services.

Business Education—for those students who want to teach business subjects at the secondary level.

THE COLLEGE OF NATURAL SCIENCES AND MATHEMATICS

This college has six departments and thirteen programs. Many of the course offerings serve as general requirements for all students in the university; a large number of the courses are for majors in the allied health programs (nursing, medical technology, and environmental health). A joint doctoral program is offered in the biological sciences in collaboration with a major research university located about thirty miles away.

The Biology Department

The biology department offers four programs and has seventeen faculty. A master's degree program is also offered.

Biology—offers an overview of the biological sciences and its various component fields such as ecology, botany, environmental science, physiology, microbiology, biostatistics, entomology, vertebrate and invertebrate biology, and cell biology.

Microbiology—the study of pathogenic and nonpathogenic bacteria, fungi, virology, and parasitology in clinical and nonclinical settings.

Wildlife Biology—the management and health of terrestrial wildlife and its environments.

Aquatic/Fisheries Biology—the management of fisheries and their habitats, pollution control, and other aspects of water and aquatic biology.

Environmental Resources—a major offering a broad overview of economic and environmental aspects of resources.

The Chemistry Department

This department consists of ten faculty offering two programs.

Chemistry—a general chemistry program containing course work in analytical, physical, and organic chemistry and biochemistry.

Chemical Technology—a two-year program preparing students for positions as laboratory technicians.

The Geology Department

This department offers three majors and a master's degree program. The programs prepare majors for careers in the petroleum, coal, and other related industries, as well as teaching at the secondary level. The majors offered are Geology, Earth Science, and a two-year program in Geological Engineering.

Mathematics and Computer Science

This twelve-member department offers majors in Computer Science, Mathematics, and Statistics. A large number of the course offerings are designed to meet general education degree requirements. The department has few math majors and is trying to cope with the specialized offerings of general statistics courses by other colleges such as Business and Law Enforcement.

The Department of Natural Sciences

This is a six-member department offering service courses which interpret the sciences to non-majors with emphasis on the historical development of the sciences and their impact on society.

The Department of Physics and Astronomy

A department of six members; physics is offered as a major along with general education courses in physics and astronomy.

THE COLLEGE OF ALLIED HEALTH AND NURSING

This college offers fourteen programs in six departments. The college has a total faculty of 37. The college departments are Emergency Medical Technology, Nursing, Health Records, Medical Technology, Environmental Health, and Occupational Health.

Emergency Medical Technology Department

One- and two-year programs offering certification in EMT, Advanced EMT, and the AA degree in EMT are available. Students are trained in techniques and management of ambulance services and accident management. There are three full-time faculty in the EMT department. Similar courses, but not a certificate or degree program, are offered in the College of Law Enforcement.

Environmental Health Department

This department has three full-time and one part-time faculty. It offers a program in Applied Biology and Chemistry with emphasis on public health aspects of pollution (air/land/noise/water), disease transmission/control, and waste disposal. Students are trained to manage these types of public health problems.

Health Records Administration Department

This department has three faculty and offers four progressively attained certifications from medical transcriptionist through the four-year health records administrator certificate and degree. The program is designed to train students in the effective management, storage, and retrieval of hospital records.

Medical Technology Department

Seven faculty offer a two-year medical assisting technology and four-year medical technology and medical laboratory technician programs. These programs are designed to train personnel to perform the medical testing in support of physician decision making, and to attain appropriate certifications (ASCAP, etc.), thus permitting employment in hospital laboratories, clinics, and other such facilities. Areas of study are hematology, clinical chemistry, clinical microbiology, parasitology, and similar subjects.

Occupational Therapy Department

This department features a four-year training program in physical therapy and has seven faculty.

Nursing

The largest department in the College, two programs are offered, leading to two- and four-year nursing degrees along with state LPN or RN certification.

ASSIGNMENT

Given the information above, your group should restructure the university to attain a maximum reduction in costs within the requirements of the Board of Regents. Your instructor will give you other directions on how to proceed.

Exercise 9   POWER AND INFLUENCE

A. POWER

A number of people have made statements about power and winning (P. T. Barnum, Mao Tse-tung, Leo Durocher, Lord Acton, Vince Lombardi, etc.). Some of these are listed below. Indicate how you feel about each of these statements by circling the appropriate number.

	Strongly Disagree	Disagree	Neutral	Agree	Strongly Agree
1. Winning is everything.	1	2	3	4	5
2. Nice guys finish last.	1	2	3	4	5
3. There can be only one winner.	1	2	3	4	5
4. There's a sucker born every minute.	1	2	3	4	5
5. You can't completely trust anyone.	1	2	3	4	5
6. All power rests in the end of the gun.	1	2	3	4	5
7. Power seekers are greedy and can't be trusted.	1	2	3	4	5
8. Power corrupts; absolute power corrupts absolutely.	1	2	3	4	5
9. You get as much power as you pay for.	1	2	3	4	5

B. INFLUENCE

During the past week or so you have come in contact with many people. Some of them have influenced you in some way—some positively ("turned you on"), some negatively ("turned you off"). Try to recall experiences you have had recently with employers, peers, teachers, parents, clergy, and the like who may have influenced you in some way. Try to think about how they influenced you and why they influenced you the way they did.

1. On the following table, list the names of all those who influenced you during the past week or so according to the kind of power that person used to influence you. The same name may appear under more than one type of social power if that person used multiple power bases to influence you. Also, indicate whether the influence was positive (+) or negative (−).

Social Power Base	Names and Whether (+) or (−)
a. Coercive:	_____
b. Monetary:	_____
c. Legitimate:	_____
d. Skill/expertise:	_____
e. Affection:	_____
f. Respect/rectitude:	_____

2. After examining your list, check (✓) the questions below.

	Yes	No
a. Was there one person who had + marks who appeared under several social power bases?	____	____
b. Was there one person who had − marks who appeared under several social power bases?	____	____
c. Did you find that most of the people with + marks tended to fall under the same power bases?	____	____
d. Did you find that most of the people with − marks tended to fall under the same power bases?	____	____

3. If you answered Yes to the last two questions, complete the following:

List those social power bases you found that were:

+   −

Do you think you personally prefer to use those power bases you listed under + when you try to influence people? Do you actually use them?

C. POWER AND INFLUENCE

From your table in Part B, find the one person who you think had the strongest positive influence on you (Person 1), and the one who had the strongest negative influence (Person 2). These are most likely the persons whose names appear most frequently (the persons you checked Yes for in the first two questions in Part B2).

On the table below, place a I on the line for each statement which best indicates how you think Person 1 would respond to each statement. Put a II on the line for each statement reflecting how you think Person 2 would respond to that item.

		Strongly Disagree	Disagree	Neutral	Agree	Strongly Agree
1.	Winning is everything.	_____	_____	_____	_____	_____
2.	Nice guys finish last.	_____	_____	_____	_____	_____
3.	There can be only one winner.	_____	_____	_____	_____	_____
4.	There's a sucker born every minute.	_____	_____	_____	_____	_____
5.	You can't completely trust anyone.	_____	_____	_____	_____	_____
6.	All power rests in the end of the gun.	_____	_____	_____	_____	_____
7.	Power seekers are greedy and can't be trusted.	_____	_____	_____	_____	_____
8.	Power corrupts; absolute power corrupts absolutely.	_____	_____	_____	_____	_____
9.	You get as much power as you pay for.	_____	_____	_____	_____	_____

Now compare your responses in Part A to those in Part C. Are you closer to Person 1 or Person 2? Do you prefer to use the kinds of power that person does? What kinds of power do you use most frequently? Which do you use least frequently? When do you feel you have the greatest power? When do you have the least power? How do these answers compare to what you found in Part B3?

Exercise 10   JOB DESIGN

This field exercise will help you understand how jobs are designed and what this may mean to those working in them.

Locate a work group in your community that will allow you to observe people at work and talk to them about their jobs. This may be in an office, a factory, a school, or the like. Using the guidelines below, come up with a job profile of the jobs within one of the work groups of the organization you visit. You should attempt to measure the jobs through observation of the employees' performance such that you can complete a job profile for the jobs you observe. If different jobs exist in the group, pick one or two which seem to be more specialized.

JOB PROFILE

Job Title   **Organization**
                                  Circle the most appropriate number

Number of motions performed	Large number of motions	7 6 5 4 3 2 1	Few motions repeated often
Number of operations performed	Large number of different operations	7 6 5 4 3 2 1	Few, repeated often
Number of different tools used to do the job	Large number	7 6 5 4 3 2 1	Small number
Human interaction	High	7 6 5 4 3 2 1	Low
Freedom and control	High	7 6 5 4 3 2 1	Low, machine-paced
Responsibility-autonomy	High	7 6 5 4 3 2 1	Low
Degree of physical exertion	High	7 6 5 4 3 2 1	Low
Environment	Pleasant	7 6 5 4 3 2 1	Unpleasant
Numbers of places work performed	Single location	7 6 5 4 3 2 1	Many locations
Location of work	Inside	7 6 5 4 3 2 1	Outside
Timing of work	Continuous/ intense	7 6 5 4 3 2 1	Intermittent

After completing the job profile, ask several of the employees how they feel about their jobs—if they are satisfied or would like to see their jobs changed in some way.

Ideally, you should ask if you can come back to talk to the employees after you do some further analysis, explained below. If this is not possible, after you have observed the work group for some time, ask employees how they feel about their jobs. For example, you could ask:

Do you like your job?

Do you think your job is routine/dull/monotonous/repetitious?

Do you find ways to add variety to your job? What are they?

If your job were to be enriched or enlarged, how would you like that? (Give them examples of additional functions they might be able to perform.)

If your job were changed in this way, would you expect to be paid more?

Again, ideally, this should be done on a second visit, if possible. Before that visit, find a job profile (if you have observed more than one kind of job) that appears to be very narrow in scope (more specialized, fewer motions, repetitive, few operations, few tools, machine paced). Develop a job redesign strategy to enlarge that person's job and reorganize the work of the work group you studied. Then make the second visit with this redesign strategy to find out employee reactions to it as outlined above. If this is not possible, you should still create a design strategy of enlargement or enrichment based on the information from your first visit.

Bring your job profiles, redesign strategy, and employee reactions (to current design and proposed redesign) to class for discussions.

 **11**

INDIVIDUAL DIFFERENCES AND ORGANIZATIONAL CULTURE

Your instructor will give you details about how to use this experience.

BEHAVIOR DESCRIPTION

Instructions: For each of the following groups of three terms, place a "3" by the term that best describes you, "1" by the term that least describes you, and "2" by the remaining term.

1. a. Adventurous _____
   b. Polished _____
   c. Stable _____

2. a. Receptive _____
   b. Determined _____
   c. Enthusiastic _____

3. a. Steady _____
   b. Exacting _____
   c. Original _____

4. a. Poised _____
   b. Patient _____
   c. Orderly _____

5. a. Forceful _____
   b. Persuasive _____
   c. Settled _____

6. a. Cautious _____
   b. Bold _____
   c. Outgoing _____

7. a. Persistent _____
   b. Cooperative _____
   c. Brave _____

8. a. Attractive _____
   b. Controlled _____
   c. Correct _____

9. a. Competitive _____
   b. Diplomatic _____
   c. Accommodating _____

10. a Careful _____
    b. Decisive _____
    c. Popular _____

11. a. Dependable _____
    b. Accurate _____
    c. Inventive _____

12. a. Convincing _____
    b. Consistent _____
    c. Open-minded _____

13. a. Positive _____
    b. Cordial _____
    c. Even-tempered _____

14. a. Conservative _____
    b. Eager _____
    c. Entertaining _____

15. a. Amiable _____
    b. Systematic _____
    c. Self-reliant _____

16. a. Sociable _____
    b. Unhurried _____
    c. Precise _____

Source: Used by permission of the author, John E. Oliver, from his article in ABSEL Proceedings, 1991.

BEHAVIOR DESCRIPTION SCORING SHEET

Instructions: Enter your scores from the Behavior Description form in the spaces below. Then add the scores in each column and enter the total for the column in the space provided.

Behavior

Dominance	Extroversion	Stability	Control
1a _____	1b _____	1c _____	2a _____
2b _____	2c _____	3a _____	3b _____
3c _____	4a _____	4b _____	4c _____
5a _____	5b _____	5c _____	6a _____
6b _____	6c _____	7a _____	7b _____
7c _____	8a _____	8b _____	8c _____
9a _____	9b _____	9c _____	10a _____
10b _____	10c _____	11a _____	11b _____
11c _____	12a _____	12b _____	12c _____
13a _____	13b _____	13c _____	14a _____
14b _____	14c _____	15a _____	15b _____
15c _____	16a _____	16b _____	16c _____
Total _____	Total _____	Total _____	Total _____

EXHIBIT 11–3

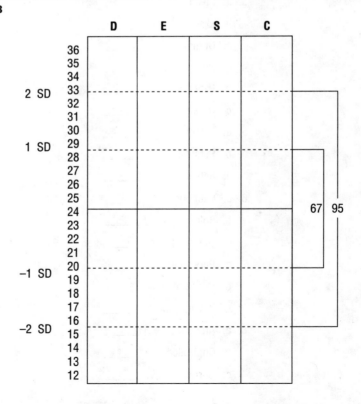

Notes:
1. The horizontal line in the middle of the graph represents the means or average scores in the normative sample.
2. Sixty-seven percent of the population is expected to score between ± 1 standard deviation (SD) from the mean.
3. Ninety-five percent of the population is expected to score between ± 2 SD from the mean.
4. Scores outside ± 2 SD are rare, indicating extreme preferences.

ORGANIZATIONAL CULTURE PROFILES

	Name of the Culture			
	Driving	Enthusiastic	Specialist	Control
Type of risks that are assumed	High	Low	High	Low
Type of feedback from decisions	Fast	Fast	Slow	Slow
The ways survivors and/or heroes in this culture behave	They have a tough attitude. They are individualistic. They can tolerate all-or-nothing risks.	They are super salespeople. They often are friendly, hail-fellow-well-met types. They use a team approach to problem solving. They are nonsuperstitious.	They can endure long-term ambiguity. They always double check their decisions. They are technically competent. They have a strong respect for authority.	They are very cautious and protective of their own flank. They are orderly and punctual. They are good at attending to detail. They always follow established procedures.
Strengths of the personnel/culture	They can get things done in short order.	They are able to quickly produce a high volume of work.	They can generate high-quality inventions and major scientific breakthroughs.	They bring order and system to the workplace.
Weaknesses of the personnel/culture	They do not learn from past mistakes. Everything tends to be short-term in orientation. The virtues of cooperation are ignored.	They look for quick-fix solutions. They have a short-term time perspective. They are more committed to action than to problem solving.	They are extremely slow in getting things done. Their organizations are vulnerable to short-term economic fluctuations. Their organizations often face cash-flow problems.	There is lots of red tape. Initiative is downplayed. They work long hours.

38

BEHAVIOR DESCRIPTION GROUP REPORT

1. Traits we have in common.

2. Strengths (things we like to do or do well).

3. Weaknesses (things we don't like to do or don't do well).

4. How will these traits, strengths, and weaknesses affect our performance and satisfaction in a work organization?

ORGANIZATIONAL CULTURE GROUP REPORT

1. Which organizational culture would provide your groups' members with the most success and satisfaction? Why?

2. List problems that might arise if all members of the organization possessed your traits, strengths, and weaknesses.

3. List some of the other types of personalities that might be needed in your chosen organizational culture and tell why they might be needed.

Exercise 12

WHO DO YOU LET GO?

The following problem is designed to give you an understanding of how groups might go about making a difficult decision and what factors mights affect that decision. There is no "correct" answer to this problem—only what each member of the group thinks is the right thing to do. The decision has several potential human resources planning and staffing implications.

You should form small study groups for this exercise and read the company background and employee descriptions. Then decide how you are to solve the problem facing the company.

BBF, INC.—COMPANY BACKGROUND

Better Business Forms, Inc. is a small manufacturer of specialty paper products used by small business firms. Their major product is printed sales vouchers custom-made for retail and dining establishments. Initially, BBF had grown quite rapidly, thus increasing production capacity and personnel. As a result of a paper shortage, BBF has had difficulty getting long-term contracts with its suppliers, and customer dissatisfaction with backlogs has increasingly become a problem. Thus, some production cutbacks are going to be necessary in the near future.

BBF is a non-union company located in an urban area where equal employment opportunity lawsuits have become quite prevalent. BBF has not had any lawsuits in this area to date, but management feels that the company is potentially vulnerable, even though the most recent employee additions have been mostly women and minority candidates.

Below are brief descriptions of six employees of BBF. Your group should make a recommendation about who should be laid off if the production cutbacks eventuate. Rank them in order of who you would let go first, second, and so on. The last person who would be laid off in this group would be ranked sixth.

BBF, INC.—EMPLOYEE DESCRIPTIONS

Charles Jefferson
Black male; age 23; veteran from Desert Storm Gulf War; married, wife pregnant; with company one year, good work record so far; capability to be better performer.

Naomi Smith
White female; age 45; recently divorced; supports 3 children; with company 5 years; number of recent absences; fairly good work record otherwise.

Robert Boyd
White male; age 20; unmarried; with company three years; good performance record; wants to start own business some day.

Ralph Ball
White male; age 45; married, no children at home; with company 10 years; erratic work record; reputed to be alcoholic.

Sarah Field
Black female; age 36; husband recently disabled; 2 children; on the job two
months; too early to evaluate performance.

Carmelita Valiquez
Hispanic female; age 41; 6 children; husband employed intermittently;
with company 9 months; steady worker; not too bright.

Exercise 13 | APPRAISING YOUR PERFORMANCE

1. Think back in your work or school experience to a time when you were performing your very best. Check (✓) the items below and indicate if they were present or absent. Also list other items not on the list which may have accounted for this high performance.

2. Now try to remember a time when you were performing poorly or at less than your best. Check (✓) the factors that were present or absent. Can you add any other factors that may have led to poor performance?

Factor	1. High Performance Present or Absent		2. Low Performance Present or Absent	
Past experience with task	_____	_____	_____	_____
Interest in the task	_____	_____	_____	_____
Expectation of reward for success	_____	_____	_____	_____
Helpful coworkers on task	_____	_____	_____	_____
Previous training for task	_____	_____	_____	_____
Strong identification with the task	_____	_____	_____	_____
Knew specifically what was expected	_____	_____	_____	_____
Superior who was interested and helpful	_____	_____	_____	_____
Felt responsible for doing the task	_____	_____	_____	_____
Participated in goals and designs of task	_____	_____	_____	_____
_____	_____	_____	_____	_____
_____	_____	_____	_____	_____
_____	_____	_____	_____	_____
_____	_____	_____	_____	_____

What can you conclude about your own performance and past successes and failures? Does this suggest anything to managers concerned about performance of subordinates? What does this mean for performance appraisal of individuals in work organizations?

Exercise 14 | EXECUTIVE CAREER DEVELOPMENT

Miriam George is the executive vice-president of a medium-sized shoe manufacturing company. She has written the following memo to her top staff members to discuss the formation of an executive development program:

> I have called a meeting for next week to develop a program for ensuring an adequate supply of executives. The problem is that we have not inventoried our own personnel resources and have failed to supply a program that encourages the development and growth of the potential executives in our organization. We need to decide on procedures for selecting our potential executives, and we need to establish a clear-cut program for preparing these people to take over.
>
> Please come to the meeting with suggestions for implementing such a program.

You have just received this memo. Your assignment is to prepare for this meeting. You will be assigned one of the following roles by the instructor:

1. Miriam George—Executive Vice-president
2. Bob Ball—V.P., Personnel
3. Ed Miller—V.P., Finance and Accounting
4. Jim Lynn—V.P., Production
5. Ralph Wiley—V.P., Marketing
6. Observer

Your instructor will give you information about each role and what each person should do for the exercise. You should prepare for a group meeting based on the instructions for your role.

Exercise 15

MOTIVATION BY MASLOW[1]

This exercise is designed to give you insights into your own needs and motivations based on Maslow's needs theory. First complete the questionnaire. When marking your responses, your answers should be based on a job you currently have (either full-time or part-time). If you have no job currently, answer according to your feelings about the last job you did have. If you have never held a job, answer in terms of the job you expect you may have when you start work.

You will be asked to compute two scores after completing the questionnaire.

QUESTIONNAIRE

Given below are several characteristics or qualities connected with your job. For each such characteristic, you will be asked to give three ratings:

a. *How much* of the characteristic is *there now* connected with your job?

b. *How much* of the characteristic do you think *should be* connected with your job?

c. *How important* is this characteristic to *you*?

Each rating will be on a seven-point scale, which will look like this:

(minimum) 1 2 3 4 5 6 7 (maximum)

You are to circle the number on the scale that represents the amount of the characteristic being rated. Low numbers represent low or minimum amounts, and high numbers represent high or maximum amounts. If you think there is "very little" or "none" of the characteristic presently associated with your job, you would circle number 1. If you think there is "just a little," you would circle numeral 2, and so on. If you think there is a "great deal, but not a maximum amount," you would circle number 6. For each scale, circle only one number. Please do not omit any scales.

1. The *feeling of self-esteem* a person gets from being in my job position:
   a. How much is there now?   (min) 1 2 3 4 5 6 7 (max)
   b. How much should there be?   1 2 3 4 5 6 7
   c. How important is this to me?   1 2 3 4 5 6 7

2. The *opportunity for personal growth and development* in my job position:
   a. How much is there now?   (min) 1 2 3 4 5 6 7 (max)
   b. How much should there be?   1 2 3 4 5 6 7
   c. How important is this to me?   1 2 3 4 5 6 7

3. The *prestige* of my job *inside* the company (that is, the regard received from others in the company):
   a. How much is there now?   (min) 1 2 3 4 5 6 7 (max)
   b. How much should there be?   1 2 3 4 5 6 7
   c. How important is this to me?   1 2 3 4 5 6 7

[1] Based on research and questionnaire developed by Lyman W. Porter. Questionnaire and data used by permission of Professor Porter.

4. The *opportunity for independent thought and action* in my position:
   a. How much is there now?   (min) 1 2 3 4 5 6 7 (max)
   b. How much should there be?   1 2 3 4 5 6 7
   c. How important is this to me?   1 2 3 4 5 6 7

5. The *feeling of security* in my job position:
   a. How much is there now?   (min) 1 2 3 4 5 6 7 (max)
   b. How much should there be?   1 2 3 4 5 6 7
   c. How important is this to me?   1 2 3 4 5 6 7

6. The *feeling of self-fulfillment* a person gets from being in my job position (that is, the feeling of being able to use one's own unique capabilities, realizing one's potentialities):
   a. How much is there now?   (min) 1 2 3 4 5 6 7 (max)
   b. How much should there be?   1 2 3 4 5 6 7
   c. How important is this to me?   1 2 3 4 5 6 7

7. The *prestige* of my job position *outside* the company (that is, the regard received from others not in the company):
   a. How much is there now?   (min) 1 2 3 4 5 6 7 (max)
   b. How much should there be?   1 2 3 4 5 6 7
   c. How important is this to me?   1 2 3 4 5 6 7

8. The f*eeling of worthwhile accomplishment* in my job:
   a. How much is there now?   (min) 1 2 3 4 5 6 7 (max)
   b. How much should there be?   1 2 3 4 5 6 7
   c. How important is this to me?   1 2 3 4 5 6 7

9. The *opportunity, in my job, to give help to other people:*
   a. How much is there now?   (min) 1 2 3 4 5 6 7 (max)
   b. How much should there be?   1 2 3 4 5 6 7
   c. How important is this to me?   1 2 3 4 5 6 7

10. The *opportunity, in my job, for participation in the setting of goals:*
   a. How much is there now?   (min) 1 2 3 4 5 6 7 (max)
   b. How much should there be?   1 2 3 4 5 6 7
   c. How important is this to me?   1 2 3 4 5 6 7

11. The *opportunity, in my job, for participation in determination of methods and procedures:*
   a. How much is there now?   (min) 1 2 3 4 5 6 7 (max)
   b. How much should there be?   1 2 3 4 5 6 7
   c. How important is this to me?   1 2 3 4 5 6 7

12. The *authority* connected with my job:
   a. How much is there now?   (min) 1 2 3 4 5 6 7 (max)
   b. How much should there be?   1 2 3 4 5 6 7
   c. How important is this to me?   1 2 3 4 5 6 7

13. The *opportunity to develop close friendships* in my job:
   a. How much is there now?   (min) 1 2 3 4 5 6 7 (max)
   b. How much should there be?   1 2 3 4 5 6 7
   c. How important is this to me?   1 2 3 4 5 6 7

In the Needs Satisfaction Table, compute your satisfaction scores. This will indicate the degree to which your job satisfies your needs.

In each case, find your answers to Parts a and b of the appropriate item from the questionnaire (e.g., 5a = How much feeling of job security is there now; 5b = How much job security should there be). Subtract a from b (b − a) and enter the score in the table below. Add up those scores and enter the sum; then divide by the appropriate number.

NEEDS SATISFACTION TABLE

	Security	Social	Esteem	Autonomy	Self-actualization
	5b − 5a =	9b − 9a =	1b − 1a =	4b − 4a =	2b − 2a =
		13b − 13a =	3b − 3a =	10b − 10a =	6b − 6a=
			7b − 7a =	11b − 11a =	8b − 8a =
				12b − 12a =	
Sum:	_____	_____	_____	_____	_____
Divide by:	1	2	3	4	3
Satisfaction score:	_____	_____	_____	_____	_____
National mean:[a]	0.43	0.33	0.61	0.78	1.05

[a] National means from Porter's sample of 1,916 managers. The numbers are "grand means" for all levels of management combined.

Compare this score to the national mean. If it is higher, your job provides less satisfaction for that particular need than jobs of a nationwide sample of managers. If it is lower than the national average, your job satisfies this need more than the jobs of the sample managers.

In the Needs Importance Table, compute your score for each of Maslow's five needs categories. These scores are derived from Part c of each item on the questionnaire. Enter each score, find the sum for each need category, and divide by the number of questions in the total.

NEEDS IMPORTANCE TABLE

	Security	Social	Esteem	Autonomy	Self-actualization
	5c =	9c =	1c =	4c =	2c =
		13c =	3c =	10c =	6c =
			7c =	11c =	8c =
				12c =	
Sum:	_____	_____	_____	_____	_____
Divide by:	1	2	3	4	3
Needs score:	_____	_____	_____	_____	_____
National mean:[a]	5.33	5.36	5.28	5.92	6.35

[a]National means from Porter's sample of 1,916 managers. The numbers are "grand means" for all levels of management combined.

Compare your needs score to the national mean. If your score is higher, that need is more important for you than for the national sample of managers. Note that managers often have a lower need for esteem and a higher need for self-actualization. Do your needs scores follow a similar pattern?

You can also compare your scores here and from the satisfaction table with the results from the national sample by level of management shown in Table A.

TABLE A

DISSATISFACTION AND IMPORTANCE OF NEEDS (BY LEVEL OF MANAGEMENT)[2]

Mean dissatisfaction[a]

			Needs		
Level	Security	Social	Esteem	Autonomy	Self-actualization
President	0.26	0.34	0.28	0.18	0.63
Vice-president	0.45	0.29	0.45	0.55	0.90
Upper middle	0.41	0.33	0.66	0.87	1.12
Lower middle	0.38	0.32	0.71	0.96	1.17
Lower	0.82	0.56	1.15	1.40	1.52

Mean importance[b]

			Needs		
Level	Security	Social	Esteem	Autonomy	Self-actualization
President	5.69	5.38	5.27	6.11	6.50
Vice-president	5.44	5.46	5.33	6.10	6.40
Upper middle	5.20	5.31	5.27	5.89	6.34
Lower middle	5.29	5.33	5.26	5.74	6.25
Lower	5.30	5.27	5.18	5.58	6.32

[a] Dissatisfaction score based on difference between obtained and expected fulfillment. Therefore, a difference score of 0 = complete satisfaction; a difference score of 6 = complete dissatisfaction.
[b] 1 = lowest degree of importance; 7 = highest degree of importance.

Compare your Needs Importance Table with your Needs Satisfaction Table. Are your most important needs being satisfied? Are your need level and satisfaction scores closer to top management or lower management? How do your results affect your behavior? Bring your results to class for discussion.

[2] Lyman W. Porter, *Organizational Patterns of Managerial Job Attitudes* (New York: American Foundation for Management Research, 1974), p. 17.

Exercise 16

BUILDING THE HOTEL SAN FRANCISCO

In this exercise you will be exposed to different leadership styles. Your instructor will divide the class into groups of approximately five members. Each group will be provided with a building kit containing a supply of computer cards, one ruler, one pair of scissors, one stapler, and a limited supply of tape. The objective is to construct the "Hotel San Francisco." The construction must have high aesthetic appeal and also be able to withstand the "big quake." (The earthquake will be simulated by dropping a book on the structure from a height of approximately five feet.)

A leader for each group will be designated. As soon as the leaders have received instructions and returned to their respective groups, the groups may begin work on their task. You will be allowed twenty minutes for construction.

When the construction period has ended, your instructor will select one person from each group to serve on a real estate appraisal board which will convene to judge each hotel on its aesthetic appeal and then conduct the earthquake simulation (book drop). Aesthetic appeal plus quake damage should be used to select the "winning" hotel. The decision of the appraisal board is final.

Your instructor will provide you with additional information for completing this exercise.

Source: Adapted from "Using Participative Management" by Samuel C. Certo, *Proceedings of the Eleventh Annual Conference of Eastern Academy of Management,* 1974. Republished in Certo and Graf, *Experiencing Modern Management,* William C. Brown Company, 1980.

Exercise 17   CHANGING WORK PROCEDURE

This is a role-playing exercise designed to give you an idea of how and why people respond as they do to changes in their work environments. Group conflict often can result when changes are introduced. A variety of forces operate in this exercise, some moving in the direction of change, others opposing it. You might try to see what the forces are and how the resistance can be reduced while positive constructive forces are generated.

Your instructor will ask you to form groups of five or six. You will be asked to select one of your members to act as the foreman, "Thompson." Three members should be selected as the crew: "Jack," "Sally," and "Walt." The fifth (and others, if present) should observe.

Now, read the case background below.

CASE BACKGROUND

You are a member of one of the compressor assembly crews working for a company which produces home air conditioners. Your work group is under the supervision of a foreman, Thompson. There are three different positions or jobs needed to assemble the compressor. Jack, Sally, and Walt work together in these positions and they can help each other from time to time. Their jobs are fairly similar, and the three change positions about every hour. (They decided to do this on their own.) Since the crew is paid on a group piece rate, the production pay is shared equally. Pieces and parts of the assembly are conveniently located next to the work bench for each of the three positions.

Just before lunch, Thompson asked Jack, Walt, and Sally to meet with him after lunch to discuss "something."

Your instructor will give you appropriate instructions for the role you are serving. Study your role in preparation for the meeting with Thompson.

The Thompsons should signal when their group members have finished studying their roles. When all the groups are ready, your instructor will set the stage for discussion to begin.

After this, you will have about twenty-five minutes to reach a decision.

Source: Adapted by Lawrence R. Jauch by permission of the author, Norman R. F. Maier, originally appearing in *Principles of Human Relations: Applications to Management*, John Wiley & Sons, Inc. (New York, 1952).

Exercise 18   EFFECTIVE LISTENING

A major problem in communications is that receivers of oral messages are not often enough in an effective listening mode. This exercise helps you understand what it means to be an effective listener.

Your instructor will ask you to read the following information and will then proceed with other directions.

INTRODUCTION

Today, modern managers know that listening is as important as, if not more important than, effective transmitting of information. How well do you think you listen? This exercise is designed to give you the opportunity to assess your listening skills and then to develop strategies to overcome listening deficiencies. Complete the parts of the exercise as directed.

Your instructor is going to give you specific instructions to follow in a few moments. Make sure you use your best listening skills.

Part A

(Complete when told to do so.)
Use your personal experience as well as what happened with others in the first part of this exercise to answer the following questions:

1. Some individuals are not successful in following instructions. Why not?

_____
_____
_____
_____
_____

2. What could the sender (in this exercise, the instructor) have done differently to increase the probability that the message would have been received more effectively (i.e., more accurately)?

_____
_____
_____
_____
_____

Part B

(Complete when told to do so.)
Develop a list of obstructions to skillful and perceptive listening.

_____
_____
_____
_____
_____

Source: Adapted from Lee Graf, "Effective Listening," *ABSEL Proceedings,* 1992, by permission

Part C

(Complete when told to do so.)

HOW DO YOU LISTEN?*
Evaluate your personal listening skills by completing this form.

Listening Habit	Almost Always	Usually	Frequency Some-times	Seldom	Almost Never	Score
Avoiding new experiences	( )	( )	( )	( )	( )	____
Faking attention to the speaker	( )	( )	( )	( )	( )	____
Avoiding difficult material	( )	( )	( )	( )	( )	____
Welcoming or creating distractions	( )	( )	( )	( )	( )	____
Finding fault with the speaker	( )	( )	( )	( )	( )	____
Listening only for details	( )	( )	( )	( )	( )	____
Getting over-stimulated by some point in the talk	( )	( )	( )	( )	( )	____
Letting bias or prejudice interfere	( )	( )	( )	( )	( )	____
Note-taking faults	( )	( )	( )	( )	( )	____
Failing to relate speaker's ideas to your own situation	( )	( )	( )	( )	( )	____

*From "Are You Sure You're a Good Listener?" *Supervisory Management* (February, 1969), pp. 33–36.

Score 2 points for Almost Always, 4 for Usually, 6 for Sometimes, 8 for Seldom, and 10 for Almost Never. A total score of 90 or above indicates an extraordinarily good listener, 70–90 a good listener, and below 60 indicates a need for listening training.

Part D

Describe what a person can do to become a (more) skillful listener.

_____

_____

_____

_____

CONTROLLING YOUR TIME

In this exercise, we want to help you analyze how you spend your time and help you develop an effective time-use plan for control purposes.

Pick a typical day next week where you will be engaged in your normal activities (classes, work, meetings, etc.). Carry the accompanying time log with you during the day from the time you wake up until you retire. When you have a chance, complete the time log by recording time spent, the activity code, with whom you spent time, who initiated the activity code, and any notes you care to make about it. Record any activity which lasts three minutes or longer.

Bring your log to class to discuss how to analyze the results and put together an effective time-use control plan. You might be thinking about ways to reorganize your schedule by recording total time spent in each classification of activity and looking at how those times compare to one another.

(Note: an alternative project of perhaps even more use is to keep a daily time log for a period of one week.)

TIME CONTROL LOG

Day of the week: _____

Time Start	End	Total Minutes	Activity	With Whom	Initiation	Action/Notes

Key

Initiation:
O—Others initiated
S—Self-initiated

Activity

P—Personal time
TT—Travel time
L—Library work
G—Group meetings
C—Class
E—Entertainment
WK—Work (job)
R—Reading/studying
W—Writing
T—Thinking
WT—Waiting time
TP—Telephone
ET—Eating

Exercise 20   FIRSTOIL COMPANY, INC.

BACKGROUND INFORMATION

This morning (Monday), Sally Green, the corporate manager of the services purchasing branch of Firstoil Company, Inc. (FCI), received a request from her supervisor, Mr. Oliver, to prepare a formal report giving the potential pros and cons of centralizing the procurement of all employee travel services. She has to present her recommendations at a purchasing department meeting that is to be held at 10 AM next Monday.

General Information

FCI, an international Fortune 500 company with $37 billion in sales last year, is based in Dallas. The company's primary business is the extraction, refinement, and distribution of POL products (petroleum, oil, and lubricants). FCI also has substantial diversified holdings.

Geographically, the U.S. region is organized into six divisions with fifty-two offices (units) employing over 25,000 people. In addition, there are two overseas divisions.

In the last two years, Firstoil had suffered sharp declines in profits due to worldwide competition and unstable oil prices. As a result, cost reduction programs were initiated throughout the company.

Purchasing Department

R. C. Oliver, manager of the purchasing department, was happy that purchasing had achieved most of its target goals in the cost reduction program. His department was organized into six branches, including the services branch which is responsible for purchasing services (such as maintenance, janitorial, architectural, construction, etc.).

More than half of all locally consumed items are purchased at either the regional or the local level. The company's president usually supported decentralization since it provided local managers with responsive and flexible service. However, centralization is utilized where significant cost savings can be obtained. For example, purchasing of most data processing equipment was recently decentralized, while deep well bits are purchased at corporate level.

Many services, such as data processing and courier service, had been centralized over the previous two years. Janitorial, building maintenance, and the hiring of temporary labor are typical of services that are still decentralized.

Security for the six divisional headquarters, some overseas locations, and corporate headquarters was recently centralized. Several months prior to negotiating for security services, Holly had surveyed all the units to gather information on the magnitude of their expenditures, categories, and type of security contracts utilized. The buying leverage gained through this information enabled her to achieve an overall upgrade in services, while reducing costs by more than 10 percent. This cost reduction was impressive since security rates were generally increasing.

Source: Adapted by the author, based on the Bestoil Company Case. Reprinted with permission from the author and publisher, the National Association of Purchasing Management, "Bestoil Company," by Dr. Roy Clinton, NAPM Case Writing in Purchasing Workshop, April 15–17, 1987.

Employee Business Travel

Following deregulation of the travel industry, Sally noticed that several companies had centralized purchasing of air travel. Some companies had negotiated favorable rates by using a more limited list of approved travel agencies. She had contemplated the feasibility of centralizing the purchasing of employee air travel, lodging, and car rentals. In light of the drop in airfares, up to 30 percent in many cases, and reduction in the price of other travel services, she wondered if significant savings could be realized in travel expenditures by centralizing this purchasing function.

During past meetings with the field purchasing agents she received negative replies on the concept. Most field purchasing agents felt that by its nature travel must be very flexible and responsive to individual needs. They pointed out that airfares were changing daily and only travel agents could arrange the best fare. Holly had read elsewhere that it was not uncommon for some city pairs to have many different rates.

Car rental rates were more consistent/standardized, however. Car rental expenditures varied significantly among the six divisions due to the different models being rented: Some executives wanted luxury sedans, while others seemed inclined to save company money by renting economy models.

The field agents felt they could also negotiate a better local lodging rate than rates obtained through a travel agent or by the corporate office. Field purchasing agents had often complained that there was some disparity in the allocation of the $37 million of travel funds and that there was no firm corporate policy covering the means and class of travel. For example, some units were sharing the travel agency commissions while others were not. In addition the commission structure varied by airline and travel agency as much as 5 percent. Some units strived to use discount fares and others paid full fares. As a group, they were using 50 different travel agencies.

There seemed to be little control above the division unit level, and total expenditures were increasing while rates were decreasing. She believed that the 11 largest units in the six U.S. divisions had 80 percent of the travel expenditures.

In a recent trade journal article, she read that the trend was toward centralizing travel services as the industry became competitive and complex. Schedules and airfares are so complex that only the national travel agencies could monitor daily changes and take advantage of those changes. Many of the smaller agencies were forced to merge with nationals in order to survive. She forwarded the article with her comments to her supervisor, which led to his request for her recommendations.

As Ms. Green sat at her desk, she wondered if there was enough time to survey the field units and prepare for the upcoming meeting. There was no internal information system that could provide a breakout of expenditures in the travel area by type of service, by category within service, or by unit. To compound the situation, comparisons would be difficult since each region or unit had its own travel standards or, in some instances, had no travel policy or standard at all. She also wondered if a centralized corporate purchasing system could enhance service and reduce costs.

MANAGEMENT INFORMATION SYSTEM TASK

Sally knew that eventually the company must develop a data base of internal and external information that could readily provide the data she needed for sound decision making. She began by listing possible types of information shown below. Your task is to design the information system you think will provide her the data she needs for this decision. To do so, follow the instructions shown on the "FCI Information Available" form.

FCI INFORMATION AVAILABLE

This page contains information Sally thought she might include for the data base. Because of cost limitations, Sally can collect only 6 categories of information. You need to tell her which categories will be most helpful for this decision.

You may examine 12 pieces of information to see what is included in the category. First, decide which 3 categories are most important. On request, your instructor will provide the information from those 3 categories for your information file. Repeat this procedure 3 more times (you will then have 12 categories of information).

From this information file your final task is to rank order the *six* categories you believe will be most useful to help Sally at her meeting next Monday. Place a 1 in the category most useful, 2 for the second most useful, and so on down through the sixth most important piece of information.

_____ 1. Financial Information on Firstoil Company, Inc.

_____ 2. Divisional Travel Budget Status

_____ 3. A Major Competitor's Expenditures by Travel Category

_____ 4. Firstoil (FCI) Expansion Plans

_____ 5. Automobile Industry Trends and Electric Cars

_____ 6. Air Travel Costs by Division

_____ 7. Environmental Concerns

_____ 8. FCI Transportation and Distribution Activities

_____ 9. Travel Agency Discounts

_____ 10. Airline Travel Tips

_____ 11. World Share of FCI Sales

_____ 12. Lodging Rate Discounts

_____ 13. Average Prices of Meals, Lodging, and Car Rentals in U.S. Geographical Regions

_____ 14. Lodging Expenditures by Division

_____ 15. FCI Domestic Oil Wells and New Oil Field Exploration

_____ 16. FCI Four-year Forecast of Prices and Profits

_____ 17. Car Rental Expenditures by Division

_____ 18. Travel Agency News

_____ 19. Japan's Car Sales

_____ 20. Average Prices of Meals, Lodging, and Car Rentals in Selected Foreign Locations

_____ 21. Domestic and Foreign Oil Reserve Holdings

_____ 22. Car Rental Agency Discounts

_____ 23. Meals and Other Travel Costs by Division

_____ 24. Weather Forecasts Affecting Air Travel

Exercise 21 | PLANNERS AND OPERATORS

This experience combines elements of planning, communication, group dynamics, and managerial interrelationships into one exercise in the context of a production activity. Clusters of ten or so people will be formed and divided into three subgroups. Four persons will serve as "planners," four as "operators," and the remaining participants will serve as "observers."

The planners will be separated and conduct a conference to decide how to instruct operators to do a task. The operators will then carry out the production as best they can while the observers watch the process, making notes of efficiencies and difficulties.

Your instructor will give you directions for completing this exercise.

Source: From Schmuck, R. A. et al. *Handbook of Organization Development in Schools* (Prospect Heights, Ill.: Waveland Press, 1992), with permission of The Center for Educational Policy and Management, University of Oregon.

INTERCULTURAL NONVERBAL COMMUNICATION

When managers interact with members of other cultures, language can be a barrier to effective communication. As important as the words is the "silent language" of nonverbal communications. Managing in a "foreign" workplace or negotiating deals can be affected. This exercise is designed to help you explore the impact of KINESICS—the effect of gestures, postures, body movement, eye contact, and spatial dimensions (interpersonal body "space").

You will be assigned to one of three roles—buyer, seller, or observer—to act out a negotiated sales contract in the international division of a microcomputer company. Your instructor will give you details about your role for this experience.

Source: Adapted from Gita Govahi and Sid Ward, "Intercultural Nonverbal Communications," *1984 ABSEL Proceedings,* pp. 221—223, by permission of ABSEL.

QUALITY AT MEMORIAL—HOSPITAL

Jim Legan is the administrator of Memorial Hospital, a secondary-level, not-for-profit hospital with 250 beds. Jim is concerned about rumors spreading around the nursing staff that there is an unusually high number of postoperative infections. Jim is not sure, but if the rumors are true, he would be quite concerned about discovering the possible source of the problem.

Jim has just finished a training program in total quality management. He decided that he would ask his assistant—you—to use one of the quality concepts to help him discover whether there was a quality control problem, and if so, what might be responsible for the infections. In his meeting with you, he relayed the following:

I would like you to prepare some Pareto charts to try to track whether we have an infection problem. J. M. Juran defined the Pareto principle which explains that 80 percent of the effects of a phenomenon are accounted for by 20 percent of the causes. A Pareto chart is a graphical tool for ranking causes from most to least significant, based on a histogram. A histogram simply lists the frequency and variation in a set of data. I think we may be able to detect the source of infections using this tool.

I have collected some data about the infections we have experienced over the last six months. Please prepare Pareto charts for frequency of infection by day, by time of day, and by operating room. As you know, our two presurgery cleaning crews rotate from operating room to operating room. Crew A does presurgery cleaning for 8:00 AM and 10:00 AM surgery procedures, and Crew B precleans for the 9:00 and 11:00 surgeries. Compare these charts and prepare a brief report for me about what you find.

Before you start your Pareto charts, you decided to check infection rates at other local hospitals. Your quality assurance nurse provided you with data from other hospitals as shown below:

POST-OP INFECTION RATES AT LOCAL HOSPITALS

#	Beds	Infections in Last Six Months	Type of Hospital
A	150	15	For profit
B	250	40	Not-for-profit

POST-OPERATIVE INFECTION INCIDENTS - MEMORIAL HOSPITAL

Day	Time of Surgery	Operating Room
F. Jan. 3	8:00 AM	1
T. Jan. 7	8:00 AM	2
T. Jan. 7	9:00 AM	3
Th. Jan. 9	8:00 AM	4
F. Jan. 10	11:00 AM	5
M. Jan. 20	8:00 AM	1
W. Jan. 22	10:00 AM	4
W. Jan. 29	10:00 AM	2
Th. Jan. 30	9:00 AM	5
F. Jan. 31	8:00 AM	5
M. Feb. 10	8:00 AM	2
M. Feb. 17	10:00 AM	3
W. Feb. 19	11:00 AM	1
Th. Feb. 20	9:00 AM	3
Th. Feb. 27	8:00 AM	5
T. Mar. 3	11:00 AM	3
M. Mar. 9	10:00 AM	4
W. Mar. 18	9:00 AM	2
F. March 27	8:00 AM	5
F. March 27	10:00 AM	5
M. Apr. 6	11:00 AM	4
M. Apr. 13	9:00 AM	3
W. Apr. 15	8:00 AM	1
F. Apr. 17	11:00 AM	5
F. Apr. 17	10:00 AM	2
T. Apr. 21	9:00 AM	2
T. Apr. 28	10:00 AM	3
W. Apr. 29	11:00 AM	4
Th. Apr. 30	10:00 AM	5
Th. May 7	8:00 AM	1
M. May 11	9:00 AM	4
T. May 12	10:00 AM	1
W. May 20	8:00 AM	3
Th. May 21	10:00 AM	2
F. May 22	9:00 AM	1
M. May 25	10:00 AM	3
T. May 26	10:00 AM	3
W. June 3	8:00 AM	4
Th. June 4	11:00 AM	1
F. June 5	9:00 AM	4
M. June 8	8:00 AM	1
M. June 15	10:00 AM	1
T. June 16	8:00 AM	2
Th. June 18	9:00 AM	5
F. June 19	11:00 AM	4
T. June 23	10:00 AM	1
F. June 26	8:00 AM	3

EFFECTIVE MANAGERS

Below is a partial list of behaviors in which managers may engage. Rank these terms in terms of their importance for effective performance as a manager. Put 1 next to the item that you think is most important, 2 for the next most important, down to 10 for the least important of these items.

_____ Communicates and interprets policy so that it is understood by the members of the organization.

_____ Makes prompt and clear decisions.

_____ Assigns subordinates to the jobs for which they are best suited.

_____ Encourages associates to submit ideas and plans.

_____ Stimulates subordinates by means of competition among employees.

_____ Seeks means of improving management capabilities and competence.

_____ Fully supports and carries out company policies.

_____ Participates in community activities as opportunities arise.

_____ Is neat in appearance.

_____ Is honest in all matters pertaining to company property or funds.

Bring your rankings to class. Be prepared to justify your results and rationale in a discussion. If you can add any behaviors to this list which might lead to success or greater managerial effectiveness, write them in.